MY FIRST
MARTIN LUTHER KING
BOOK

by Dee Lillegard
illustrated by Helen Endres

created by The Child's World

CHILDRENS PRESS ®
CHICAGO

Library of Congress Cataloging in Publication Data

Lillegard, Dee.
    My first Martin Luther King, book.

    1. King, Martin Luther—Juvenile literature.
2. Afro-Americans—Biography—Juvenile literature.
3. Baptists—United States—Clergy—Biography—
Juvenile literature.   I. Endres, Helen.
II. Child's World (Firm)   III. Title.
E185.97.K5L48   1987   323.4'092'4   [B]   86-31670
ISBN 0-516-02908-8

MY FIRST
MARTIN LUTHER KING
BOOK

Three Boys

Three little boys in Atlanta
Used to play together a lot.
Two of them were white,
And one of them was not.

One day the white boys' parents
Met the black boy at their door
And said, "You cannot play
With our sons anymore."

The black boy's mamma hugged him
And told him, "Never forget.
You are as good as anyone.
They just don't know it yet."

M·L·

M.L. was what they called him.
He played with all his might.
Some kids said he played too hard.
And he liked to fight.

He would wrestle anyone,
No matter what his size.
But he'd fight fair and often win—
To everyone's surprise.

When M.L. grew older,
He led the *peaceful* fights—
With words and songs and marching
That helped win *civil rights*!

8

Shoes

New shoes!
New shoes for my feet!
I am going to walk
Up and down the street. . .
In my brand new shoes,
M.L. thought.
But on that day
No shoes were bought.

Daddy was proud
That he was black.
He left the store—
Wouldn't move to the back.

The white man said
That's what Daddy had to do.
But he *didn't*. And M.L.
Felt proud, too!

Bicycle

M.L. had a dream
That he had a new bike,
A brand new bike of his own.
So he went right out
And got a paper route.
He worked real hard—all alone.

He had to deliver
Those papers all over.
But it was something he was glad to do—
Because he knew
That was how
He'd make his dream come true!

Words!

"I'm going to get me some big words!"
M.L. said.
He couldn't get enough big words
in his head.

He liked to read them, write them,
weigh them—
But best of all he liked
to *say* them!

Books

Martin Luther King loved books.
He loved reading and thinking.
He read the words of the Bible
And of Abraham Lincoln.

He remembered what he read,
And he liked to recite.
He read a whole *mountain* of books!
Then *he* began to write.

A Voice

All by himself—
When M.L. was very small,
He sang in front of his daddy's church.
He sang very well.

As M.L. grew older,
His voice grew deep and strong.
His people loved to hear him speak,
And sing a special song.

"We shall overcome," he said—
"All hurtful thoughts—some day.
Then boys and girls of *all* colors
Can come together and play!"

Football

Zoom! Crash!
There went M.L.
He could run real hard,
And if he fell,

He'd get up again
Because *he* had a dream
That he was going to win
For his whole team.

No one could stop him—
He had a plan.
He was that kind of boy
And that kind of man.

Coretta

When Martin was a young man,
He met a pretty lady named Coretta.
She was a leader, too.
And she was right for him—he knew.

When Coretta first met Martin, *she*
Thought, *Oh, he isn't very tall.*
But as she got to know him,
That didn't matter at all!

A Leader

He was a man who liked to laugh—
Sometimes he would tease.
He loved to eat good "soul" food—
Like pork and black-eyed peas.

He was a man who loved his family.
He was kind to all he knew.
And Martin Luther King was a *leader*—
His fame grew—and grew.

The whole world was watching him,
Watching his star rise.
One day this peaceful leader won
The *Nobel Peace* prize!

24

A Dream

What is a dream?
Does it only come at night—
When you're fast asleep
And the covers are tight?

Some dreamers have dreams
Wide awake, through the day.
When they share their dreams,
People listen to what they say.

Dr. King had a dream
That was wonderful to hear.
He dreamed that the great day
Of freedom was near—
And he told his dream
To the world—*loud and clear*!

DR. M.L. KING JR.

I HAVE A DREAM

1963

LINCOLN MEMORIAL

Bus Ride

The bus is long enough—
And wide—
For all of us
To fit inside.

The bus is ours—
It's yours and mine.
We can ride it,
Feeling fine.

Why not try it?
Let's all ride,
Black and white—
Side by side.

Color

If you see a giraffe
And it makes you laugh,
What does the color of your skin
    have to do with it?

If you stub your toe,
It hurts, you know.
What does the color of your skin
    have to do with it?

Your skin is only a coat you wear—
Over the rest of you.
Inside—where yourself is—*there*
Is the best of you!

Freedom

For all people,
For all races,
For all our different
Shapes and faces—

For rich or poor,
For high or low,
Let's have freedom
Wherever we go!

Freedom at last!
Let freedom ring!
These were the words
Of *Martin Luther King.*